HONG KONG PANORAMAS the little book of big pictures

From the greenery of The Peak to the dramatic towers of glass dominating Victoria Harbour, Hong Kong dazzles with a unique combination of natural beauty and man-made enterprise. Yet away from the business monoliths lies a Chinese city of narrow streets, old shop houses selling a myriad obscure commodities, and temples to revered local gods, all surrounded by countryside with islands and feng-shui woods where the old way of life is still preserved.

Published by Pacific Century Publishers Ltd.
Copyright and Text © 2008 Pacific Century Publishers

Photographs © Fumio Okada
ISBN 978-988-98125-6-0

Pacific Century Publishers Limited
Suite 1603-4, Hon Kwok Jordan Centre
7 Hillwood Road, Tsimshatsui
Kowloon, Hong Kong

Tel: (852) 2376 2085   Fax: (852) 2376 2137
Email: pacman@pacificcentury.com.hk
Website: www.pacificcentury.com.hk

Printed in Hong Kong / China

The Star Pisces cruise ship navigates the narrow Lei Yue Mun Channel as it enters Victoria Harbour from the east. Behind are the villages of Ma San Tsuen and Lei Yue Mun, famous for its seafood restaurants. *(previous page)*

SKYSCRAPERS OVER HONG KONG

Land is now so scarce in Hong Kong that the only way to go is up! State-of-the-art residential spires on Stubbs Road, Hong Kong Island, overlook the glass and steel towers of the Central Business District including Hong Kong's highest building, '2IFC', the 88-storey Two International Finance Centre (right). In the distance, the hills of Lantau Island.

HONG KONG'S HARBOUR AT NIGHT One of the true wonders of the world, the unforgettable sight of
Hong Kong's Victoria Harbour as seen from The Peak. This land-locked harbour endowed
Hong Kong with its original worth, the perfect place for an entrepôt port linking the West
with the sleeping giant – China. The illuminated real estate bears witness to its continued success.
(previous page)

MAN MO TEMPLE Situated on Hollywood Road in Central, the Man Mo Temple is built on traditional lines and dedicated to two Taoist deities: Man Cheong, the god of literature, and Mo Kwan Kung, the martial god. Visitors are usually more interested in the profusion of giant incense coils that hang from the ceiling.

VICTORIA HARBOUR AND WANCHAI
Central Plaza, Asia's one-time tallest building, dominates the North Wanchai waterfront with the wing-like roof of the Hong Kong Convention and Exhibition Centre located on reclaimed foreshore.

THE HARBOUR AT NIGHT
In this time-release shot, ripples of light show how busy Victoria Harbour remains at night as ferries and commercial craft ply their trade. Meanwhile in Hong Kong's commercial buildings beneath Victoria Peak, traders work late talking to other financial centres in time zones beyond the west horizon.

STAR FERRY AT SUNSET As the Star Ferry steams past the Wanchai waterfront on its regular crossing from Hung Hom in Kowloon to Hong Kong Island, the setting sun catches the glass curtain wall of 78-storey Central Plaza, making it gleam like a dazzling jewel reflected in the harbour.

TRAM Two of Hong Kong's 100-year-old trams, modernized of course, wind their way eastwards past the Legislative Council Building in Central District. One of the longest-serving components of Hong Kong's amazing transport system, trams are a non-polluting and, for many Hong Kong working people, a highly affordable mode of transport, remaining in service by popular demand. Trams are available for private hire as well as advertising. *(previous page)*

STANLEY Many expatriates live in Stanley, which is also a mecca for tourists who come to its famous market in search of clothing and Chinese handicrafts. A number of Western-style pubs have opened along Stanley Main Road to cater to this clientele; Chinese customers are few here. Access is convenient since the construction of a tourist complex and carpark at the end of this cul-de-sac.

WANCHAI MARKET This is one of the main traditional "wet markets" where raucous stall-holders sell fresh meat, fish, fruit and vegetables. Traditionally, Hong Kong people have always bought their food fresh each day and many people still prefer the old way, despite the availability of convenience shopping in supermarkets.

JUMBO FLOATING RESTAURANT

The famous floating Jumbo Restaurant and its neighbour, Tai Pak Seafood, are familiar tourist landmarks in the Aberdeen typhoon shelter. Originally there was a third restaurant, which was supposedly shipped to Manila, although it is nowhere to be found in the Philippines.

VICTORIA HARBOUR FROM CENTRAL   A traditional Chinese junk plies the harbour. Behind (left) is the Cultural Centre located on the tip of the Kowloon peninsula and (right) the Hong Kong Convention and Exhibition Centre, Causeway Bay and North Point beyond. *(previous page)*

PENINSULA HOTEL Privileged diners on the Sun Terrace of the Peninsula Hotel in Kowloon enjoy not only a sumptuous dinner, but also a magnificent view of Hong Kong Island by night. The Peninsula, opened in 1928, is one of the grand old hotels of Asia, famed for its elegant, high-ceilinged lobby which is the best place in Hong Kong to have tea.

CRUISE LINERS AT THE OCEAN CROSSROADS As the gateway to China, Hong Kong is a major hub and port of call on the cruise liner circuit in the Orient. Liners berthed at the Ocean Terminal disgorge their well-heeled patrons into the shopping mecca of Tsim Sha Tsui, while US Navy vessels still pay courtesy calls to Hong Kong as they have done since the Second World War.

TSIM SHA TSUI   The colourful streets of Tsim Sha Tsui, at the tip of the Kowloon peninsula, offer both
tourists and locals every kind of shop, service, restaurant and entertainment imaginable. Traffic congestion
is a problem in what is one of the most densely populated urban areas in the world.

NATHAN ROAD, KOWLOON   The main artery of Kowloon which runs due north from the waterfront, busy Nathan Road is known as Hong Kong's "Golden Mile". This is the heart of the hotel and tourist area, with brilliant neon signs advertising a host of shops, restaurants, karaoke centres and girlie bars.

TAI KOK TSUI   These brightly coloured barges at Tai Kok Tsui, near Kwai Chung, contribute greatly to the efficiency of the container port. Their powerful cranes are used to offload containers from ocean-going ships moored in the harbour to the shore. Often the crew live on board. Sampans are still in use as water taxis.

SHATIN RACECOURSE Horse-racing is Hong Kong's most popular spectator sport. Thousands flock to both Happy Valley, where meetings have been held since 1846, and Shatin, the Jockey Club's newer venue, during the season. Racing is the territory's only legal form of gambling and huge sums are regularly wagered. *(previous page)*

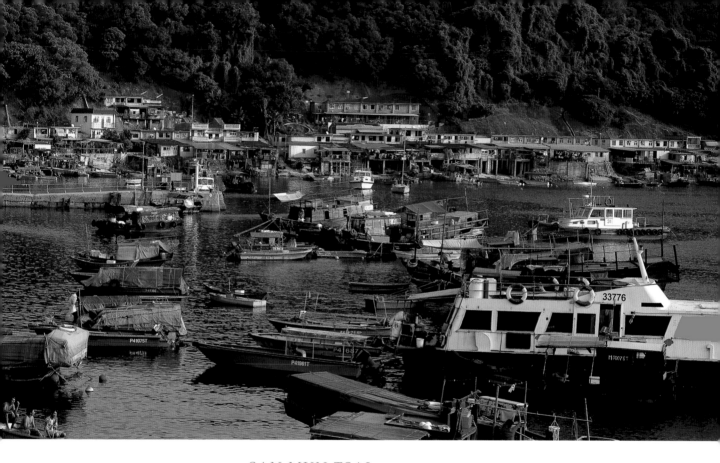

SAN MUN TSAI The traditional way of life survives in this ancient fishing
village near Tai Po, in the northeast New Territories, where some 300 residents
of Tanka descent still live in houses built on piles over the water.

DWELLINGS ON MA WAN ISLAND

Representatives of a rapidly vanishing way of life, many families on the small island of Ma Wan still live in "home-made" dwellings on stilts above the water. Located off the northeast extremity of Lantau Island, Ma Wan now lies in the shadow of the Kap Shui Mun Bridge and the Tsing Ma Bridge, which together link Lantau with Tsing Yi and the New Territories beyond.

LAM TSUEN WISHING TREE This ancient banyan tree in Tai Po is festooned with red and gold incense papers at Chinese New Year. People write their wishes on a "bao die", a strip of yellow paper, tie the paper to an orange, and then try to throw it onto the tree. Chinese people are superstitious and believe that if it lands on a branch, the gods will grant their wishes. *(previous page)*

TSING CHUNG KOON TEMPLE   Taoism is the most ancient religion in Hong Kong, pre-dating Buddhism
and Christianity. This beautiful Taoist temple in Tuen Mun, in the northwest New Territories,
was once in a serene setting of natural woodland but now is surrounded by a concrete jungle of
high-rise residential estates.

TSING CHUNG KOON TEMPLE
Perhaps the mostly richly decorated interior of any Taoist temple in Hong Kong. Tsing Chung Koon boasts an imposing central altar for the main Chinese deity, flanked by two other deities. Ornately carved and decorated panels, inscribed pillars, elaborate textiles and lanterns are all in perfect symmetry.

JOSS STICKS PAR EXCELLENCE These super-size joss sticks perfume the air at the Po Lin Monastery on Lantau Island. Home of the world's largest outdoor bronze seated Buddha, Po Lin is the spiritual centre of Hong Kong, with pilgrims from Asia and beyond flocking to see its Buddha. A cable car from Tung Chung town will soon shorten the journey up to the monastery.

SHA TAU KOK Looking across Sha Tau Kok Hoi from Nam Chung, it is clear that over the past 30 years, the pace of modern development has been much faster on the mainland Chinese coast than on the Hong Kong side of the border. However, it seems certain that this peaceful rural idyll cannot exist for much longer.

SOK KWU WAN   In late afternoon sunshine, pleasure junks bring visitors to the well-known seafood restaurants of the village of Sok Kwu Wan, on the north shore of Lamma Island. Villagers breed and keep fish and seafood to supply the restaurants in fish rafts seen in the foreground. *(previous page)*

TING KAU BRIDGE Providing a link from Tsing Yi Island, via the Tai Lam Tunnel and Route 3 highway to the Chinese border, Ting Kau Bridge also connects with the Tsing Ma Bridge leading to Hong Kong International Airport. By night it seems to be transformed from a mere bridge into a magnificent work of sculpture.

TSING MA BRIDGE A last brilliant ray of light from the setting sun illuminates the Tsing Ma Bridge in all its splendour. Part of the Lantau Link connecting urban Hong Kong with the new airport at Chek Lap Kok, this is the longest road and rail traffic suspension bridge in the world with pylons over 200 metres high and a main span of 1,377 metres. *(previous page)*

HONG KONG INTERNATIONAL AIRPORT

Old and new make a striking contrast at Hong Kong International Airport at Chek Lap Kok. On display is a replica of the Farman Biplane, the first aircraft to fly in Hong Kong in 1911. The 550,000-square-metre terminal, designed by Sir Norman Foster, is the world's largest enclosed public structure, handling 45 million passengers and 3 million tonnes of cargo per year.

CHI LIN NUNNERY The simple beauty and harmony of these grey ceramic tiled roofs above the timber construction of the temple buildings demonstrates the solemnity of traditional Buddhist architecture - in sharp contrast with the highly coloured Taoist temples in Hong Kong.

CHINESE OPERA

Hong Kong's ethnic roots live on in performances of traditional Chinese folk opera, usually staged outdoors on temporary bamboo sets with no admission charge. This drama celebrates the annual Hungry Ghosts Festival in July, during which ancestors' spirits are believed to return and are offered food by the living. *(previous page)*

Hong Kong is a place of peculiarly Chinese festivals celebrating such events as Lunar New Year, Dragon Boat Festival, Hungry Ghost Festival, or honouring Tien Hou, the goddess of fishermen. The lion dance is often seen at these times as well as on more prosaic occasions such as the opening of a new department store or restaurant when they help drive away evil spirits and ensure good business.

SEA OF ORCHIDS The Flower Festival held in Victoria Park at Lunar New Year always attracts legions of horticultural connoisseurs. It also attracts many flower vendors who pay astronomical prices at auction to guarantee themselves a stall in the limited space available at the festival. In addition to orchids, seasonal favourites include peach trees in full blossom and kumquat bushes.

KOWLOON AND CENTRAL, C.1950 Panorama photographs are not a new phenomenon. This shot shows how the Victoria Harbour panorama looked 50 years ago, taking in Tsim Sha Tsui and the Peninsula Hotel. In the foreground stand the former Hong Kong Bank building and, to its right, the Bank of China building with, to its right, the old cricket ground, now Chater Garden.